In God's Waiting Room

by

Ernestine Carreker

Forward by
Deborah A. Wright

In God's Waiting Room

Printed in the United States of America

ISBN 978-0-9843245-1-4

Published by Parablist Publishing
P.O. Box 43379
Richmond Heights, OH 44143

Website: www.parablistpublishinghouse.com
Email: parablistpublishing@yahoo.com

Forward

"In God's Waiting Room", takes an inside look at the arduous seven year emotional roller coaster of events surrounding Ernestine Carreker's divorce from her husband, an Associate Minister at her Church. Ernestine describes through recollection and in her journal entries, the hurt and deception of being married to a Minister, active in the Church, yet victimized simply because she chose to trust in the Lord and allow Him to fight her battles. In addition to the physical and emotional abuse suffered by her husband, she suffered abuse from the legal system that failed her, the daughter that betrayed her and the ongoing economic battle that constantly threatened her day-to-day existence.

"In God's Waiting Room", will encourage readers to trust in the Lord and do good. Ernestine is a living example that if we hold our peace, God will fight our battle, but we MUST wait on the Lord. Through her recollection and journal entries, she shares her heartache, pains and eventual victory. Ernestine's story gives voice to the silent tears and pain of women in similar situations. Through her story, you can peek, first hand inside God's waiting room.

Deborah A. Wright

Publisher/CEO Parablist Publishing House

Dedications

I thank God for some very special people in my life, who helped me in various ways. Special thanks go to Bishops Sheri and Gregory Collins, Pamela Carreker, Sheronda Brown, Cassandra Johnson, Celeste Smith, Darlene Stitmon, Eddie Strattonbey, Michelle Strattonbey, Brenda Dove, Erica Witherspoon and Denise Lewis.

There were so many others, who supported and encouraged me in various ways during this period of my life. I wish to thank you all. Last but certainly not least, to my middle daughter. My prayer is that we may one day see eye-to-eye, but until then, know that I love you.

These people draw near to Me with their mouth, and honor Me with their lips, but their heart is far from Me.

Matthew 5:8

"Even though I grew up in Church, I can honestly say that I did not know who God really was or how to have a real relationship with Him. I knew there was something more and I could not stop until I found out what it was."

Table of Contents

Chapter One

About Me…

I was born on April 11, 1951 in Jackson

Mississippi. My mother and stepfather moved to Cleveland, Ohio when I was only five years old.

Growing up, even as a young child, I took care of my sisters and brothers. I was quiet, yet caring. I always tried to put the needs of other people before my own. I love to spend time listening to and gleaning wisdom from older people. I am known as a giver and whatever I do, I have a passion for being on time.

It was instilled in me from my youth to go to Church, but at the time, I did not feel like I had a real relationship with God. Even though I attended Church and went through the motions, I always felt like there was more. I wanted to learn about God and have a personal experience with Him. My heart yearned for a deeper relationship with God.   I often wondered, "What did God really want of me?" Looking back at my life, these were my seeking years.

After graduation, I worked part-time at the Post Office. One day after work, one of my best friends was going out with her boyfriend. She suggested that I join them. They had invited a friend named John. They wanted me to meet him.

Right away, I did not like him. He was arrogant; he looked at women as if they were beneath him. I tried to be polite and get through the blind date as gracefully as possible. He asked me for my phone number. Reluctantly, I gave it to him, (hoping all the while that he would not call.)

Later on, John told me that he thought I had purposely given him the wrong number. He had tried it and evidently had dialed the wrong number. Looking back, I wish I had given him the wrong number or that he had given up after the mis-dial. He didn't. We ended up going out to dinner. The dinner and everything was o.k., but it was still hard to connect with him.

Trying to be polite, I invited him to Church. I guess in his way, he was trying to be polite and agreed to come. He attended but it was very clear that he did not want to be there. We spent some time together. It still felt awkward. We were in two different worlds.

As time went on, he began to realize that I was not like the other girls he was used to dating. He desperately tried to change my principles, I held true to who I was. We stopped seeing each other. John left to go back to the Army. I thought it was all over and went on with my life.

The next year John returned home from the Army. Shortly after arriving home, he called me. At the time, I was seeing someone else, but it was nothing serious so I agreed to go out with him. We went out and talked. For the first time, we connected a bit. He told me that he had a year to think through all that had transpired between us. He said that he had never dated anyone quite like me. He was used to having his way with women. They did whatever he requested and he just did not know how to handle me. He had realized that there was something intriguing in that difference and he wanted to marry me.   Now tell me, what woman doesn't yearn to hear the words…I am different…you want to marry me? Boaz, Prince Charming,…most women dream of this.

Words are sometimes are just empty syllables. I did not have a deep enough relationship with God, to ask Him first for a husband. I was not deep enough with God to see through those words. Every woman wants to hear those words, and every man knows that! Sometimes, we fall for the hype. I looked past having someone who loved God first and would love me the way they loved God. Looking back, I clearly see now that a happy marriage takes more than just loving God for yourself. A happy marriage is a three-fold cord, God, the husband and the wife.

John and I got married August 15, 1970. We had our first baby on February 25th. We bought our first house shortly after that. Our second daughter was born on November 30th.

During this time in our lives, we were happy. John did not go to Church much, but I continued to take the girls.

We had some good times as a family. We went on nice vacations and John and I enjoyed the life we had with the girls, In spite of all we shared together, John still felt the need to go out in the world. Over time, he continued drinking and going out. I prayed so much for him to come out of the streets.

I did not like going out much at all, but sometimes I would go just to try to keep the peace at home. I always felt like I was in the wrong place. I would go with him and order water with lemon. He seemed to be having such a great time. I was uncomfortable and bored. I stopped trying to please him and go out with him, and stayed home.

Let your fountain be blessed, and rejoice with the wife of your youth. As a loving deer and graceful doe, let her breasts satisfy you at all times; and always be enraptured with her love. For why should you, my son, be enraptured by an immoral woman, and be embraced in the arms of a seductress?

Proverbs 5:18-20

*W*hat more can be said? John left his first love to embrace and enter into an adulterous relationship with a strange woman. How unpleasing in the sight of God.

Chapter Two

The Other Woman

I became pregnant with our third daughter, eight

years into our marriage. Before our youngest daughter was

born, John went to a picnic with his job and took the two

oldest girls. He felt it was better if I did not go, so I stayed

home. After the picnic, the girls came home and said,

"Mommy, Daddy took us to the picnic with his girlfriend".

What news! I was eight months pregnant. and two weeks

away from maternity leave. I said nothing to him on that

Friday and he went to work as usual. I packed my bags and

the girls and I flew to Jackson, Mississippi to my father's

house.

I told my mother-in-law what happened and she

agreed that I should go. I wrote him a note and I left.

I arrived in Mississippi late Friday night. My mother-in-law told me that when he came home, his plan was to go out that night. He had cleaned the car, (it was green) put on his green suit and was ready to run the streets. My mother-in-law said instead of going out he ended up staying home. He told her that he needed to talk, She told him he need to stay out of the streets.

He called me, but I refused to talk to him. I had so much on my mind, the girls, the new baby, the lady. It was a lot for anyone, let alone a wife nine months pregnant. When I refused to listen to him, he got in his green car and drove eighteen hours straight to Jackson, Mississippi.

I listened to his crying. I listened to his lies. I felt that I had very few options but to give our marriage another try. I came home a week later. Shortly after I came home, I had the baby. It was another precious baby girl.

After the new baby and as part of his attempt at restoring our marriage, John started going back to Church with us again.

I appreciated his attempt, but it was quite evident that he was there in body, but not in spirit.

Soon after this reconciliation attempt, John got laid off from his job. A lot was going on during this time. I was the only one working and my mother-in-law passed away. This was a very stressful time. She was the best mother-in-law I could ever ask for. She was my friend. We talked about everything. There were times she could not even talk to her son. I valued and appreciated our relationship. We looked out for each other. When my mother-in-law died, John's sister and brother needed a place to stay, I was there when no other family stepped in. His step dad drank a lot and the kids stayed with us until his brother went to the Army and his sister got married. I really missed my mother-in-law. She helped me through some rough times.

*A*nd the Word of the LORD came to me, saying, "Son of man, prophesy against the shepherds of Israel, prophesy and say to them, "Thus says the Lord God to the shepherds: "Woe to the shepherds of Israel who feed themselves! Should not the shepherds feed the flocks? You eat the fat and clothe yourselves with the wool; you slaughter the fatlings, but you do not feed the flock.

Ezekiel 34:1-3

"My husband went from the pew to the pulpit with his own agenda. Leaders must be careful not to promote themselves at the expense of shattered and broken people. When giving attention to their own needs and ideas instead of God's, they push aside and abandon those who depend on and trust them."

Chapter Three

John joins the Church

*O*ne day I came home from Church and John's best friend had invited him to his Church. When I came home, John excitedly told me that he had joined the Church. I remember that moment so well. I was cooking, the kids were playing, but everything went silent at his announcement.

I was so happy. I thanked God. John got baptized and so did our youngest daughter. The girls and I, changed Churches to be with him. We later changed to another Church that John felt was a better place for us to grow spiritually as a family. . I joyfully, stayed with John. We were finally in Church together as a family. Wherever he wanted to go was fine with me.

After a year or two, John announced to us that he felt he had been called to preach.

For a while, things were great, the reconciliation of our marriage, the new Church and now the new call upon John's life. It all seemed so perfect. Of course, that is when the devil loves to re-enter the picture. Before, John's temptations were coming from the world with his clubbing and going out. At first, I thought it was my imagination. The devil told me it was all in my mind. Surely, this can not be happening in the Church! To my surprise, it was. Women were chasing him, or he was chasing them, just like in the streets. It was not just my imagination. John did not even have to go to the streets. He could play the field right from the pews of the Church.

I brought up my suspicions to him. Of course, he denied it, covered it up and tried to play it off. In his efforts to play it off, he bought a new house to take my focus off of what was going on.

The first year we were there, I was not happy. I realized what it was all about. The feelings and suspicions I was having could not be quieted with material possessions. It was just a house. It takes so much more to make a house a home. I desired a home. A home for my husband and our girls. No matter, what he bought me to dress up the house, it was still just a house.

So many things were given to me by John take my focus off the truth,. Each time I knew something was not right. I tried, but could not talk to him. In his eyes, he knew everything, especially, when it came to the Word of God. I would ask him to show me where what he was saying was in God's Word. His attempts to answer made me sick in the stomach. How could he make up such lies and say it was God's Word? I began to worry because I knew things were not right and were steadily getting worse.

I had to have an operation due to an ulcer in my stomach. I ended up having part of my stomach removed. During the surgery, John left the hospital. He said the surgeons were taking too long. Later, I found out that I had died on the operating table, but the doctors were able to revive me. God said not yet. I was alive, living with half a stomach and John was no doubt disappointed.

We began building a new house. It was nice watching it being built and I was happy and thanked God for it. In the back of my mind and in my heart I longed for happier times with my husband and family. When we moved into our new house, unpacked all of the fixings of our life together, I somehow thought something would miraculously transfer the house into a home. . Once all of the belongings were neatly positioned in their place, even though it was nice, it still felt like something was missing. No matter what he did to cover things up, the house never felt like home. I never felt the joy and love that comes with a home. I continued to love and care for my family and my new house, all the while feeling the emptiness inside of me.

I continued to do what I had done since a child, take care of everyone else. I had begun to draw close to God and do the things I thought would move me up in holiness. I put myself last. I loved my family, I remained quiet and reserved waiting patiently for something more. There had to be more. More to life than this emptiness that filled me inside. My suspicions were no longer suspicions, John was having another affair.

This was a devastating time in my life. I needed and sought much healing, just to cope day-to-day. I had so many unanswered questions. I was like so many hurting women not knowing what to do concerning their situation. The questions were many. "Where do I go from here?" "I attend Church faithfully, I serve God but why me?" "Should I take revenge for my sorrow?" I even had someone tell me that there was no way out but to kill myself.

Thank God, I knew better. I knew enough to know that God sends refuge for the brokenhearted. God tells you to look to the hills where your help comes from. God tells us that vengeance is His and that He will repay your enemy for their actions.

"No one, when he has lit a lamp, covers it with a vessel or puts it under a bed, but sets it on a lamp stand, that those who enter may see the light. "For nothing is secret that will not be revealed, nor anything hidden that will not be known and come to light."

Luke 8:16-17

*"**O**n August 23, 2002 the scriptures, Luke 8:16-17 became very real to me. It is amazing the avenues the Lord will use to open your eyes to situations. What an awesome and faithful God we serve! Even when we don't know what we need, He does."*

Chapter Four

The Stranger

*I*t was August 23, 2002. Early in the morning,

God started revealing something to me. He revealed to me
that there was something about that lady from New York
my husband had been calling continually. I would ask him
about her, he denied knowing anything about it. . Later on
that very day, my daughter invited me to a bridal shower.
On the way to the bridal shower, someone in another car
driving along beside us and called out my name. This
person seemed to know me, but I didn't know him,. He
asked us to pull over. Somewhat afraid, we did. This
stranger proceeded to tell me things about my life. He
knew I had three children, how long I had worked at my
job. He also knew one of my children had a hearing loss
and that I had recently filed for divorce. I was in shock by
all that he revealed. He proceeded to tell me where my

husband was at that very moment. He was with another woman. My heart sunk and my head was spinning at all I had just heard. I knew the woman he was talking about. I knew her because I took supplies over to her house when my husband was installing her kitchen. I knew "Liz". My daughter heard the entire conversation. She was afraid and said, "Mommy, I'm not going over this woman's house, because Daddy is going to kill somebody".

After all that the stranger shared with me, I wanted to find out for myself, but was not sure if it was the right thing to do. I went over to the house of a trusted friend of mine. I shared all that the stranger had shared with me. She spoke words of wisdom to me and said, "Baby, I want to know if this is from God or is the devil trying to spew lies to hurt you". We decided to go to Liz's house and see first-hand.

When we arrived at Liz's house, we could see them through the window. My husband was sitting there relaxed and comfortable. They were sitting knee-to-knee as if they were on a date. When they saw us at the door, they jumped up in shock. They tried to act as if nothing was happening. I was hurt. I started crying. John tried to place the blame on my friend. He asked her why she would bring me over to hurt me like that.

I wanted so badly to hit Liz. I wanted her to hurt like I was hurting, but my arms wouldn't move. Liz tried to defend herself by saying that my husband was only there to counsel her. She enjoyed his counsel because he was so easy to talk to. She also revealed that it was her birthday.

When my husband found out about the stranger who had shared this information with me, he threatened to kill him. Tony, the man who had told me about my husband, was a married man. He and Liz had been having an affair for twelve years of his marriage .

My husband went out looking for Tony. When he finally came home, he tried to explain that nothing was going on. He told lies to cover lies. Everything that came out of his mouth was lies. I was so scared and confused. I did not know what I was going to do.

I thanked God for Tony. God wanted me to see the truth for myself. I had felt for a long time that something was going on. When I confronted him, he would say that I was losing my mind and a fierce argument would begin. He denied and denied all the while maintaining and defending his constant contact with Liz.

The devil began to torment my mind. The taunts of my husband echoed the taunts of the devil. They taunted me, telling me that my only way out was to do harm to myself. They told me to go lay down on the freeway or take a knife to my heart and end it all. I had enough God in me to know better than listen to the devil or John. It felt like a knife pierced my heart every time my husband would spew such hateful and disrespectful words.

I struggled to keep my mind. The only way I knew to do this was keep my mind on the Lord. I continued to go to Church and fill my heart with the Word of God. I would tell the devil that God would not be pleased if I took matters in my own hand. I had to keep reminding myself that my life was in God's hands.

One night, while watching a service where T. D. .Jakes was preaching. I felt that the message that night was directly to me. He said that God wants me to stand. I received strength from that Word. It gave me courage. It gave me strength to carry on.

Trust in the LORD with all your heart, and lean not on your own understanding; In all your ways acknowledge Him, and He shall direct your paths.

Proverbs 3:5-6

"When we have an important decision to make, we should consult our Heavenly Father and not depend on our own independent thinking. As our Creator, He knows what is best for us. We should always be ready to listen and accept His righteous judgements."

Chapter Five

Threats and Promises

I sought counseling with a Pastor. My husband did

not want to attend counseling with me. I cried out to God.

I needed Him to lead me in the right direction. I was so

hurt and confused. What was I to do? After some time,

John finally decided to attend counseling with me. As we

both attended counseling together, John continued to

defend himself, by saying that he would continue

counseling Liz.

One time, during one of the counseling sessions,

John exploded and even threatened to kill me!   The

counselor reported this to the police.

John defended his actions by continuing to say that I was crazy for believing such things could be true about him. He said that I was just jealous of all of the women that he often spoke with and counseled daily.

For John, this now made two threats. After Tony had told me what was going on, John threatened to kill him too.

John went to court, but because it was his word against ours, Minister John wiggled out of all of the charges against him.

Hurt and confused, again, I started standing on the Word of God. I called out to God. I needed to know what to do.   My husband did not seem to care about anything. He definitely did not care about me or about our marriage. He was adamant about maintaining his counseling arrangement with Liz. He denied that Liz was his girlfriend, but he emphatically declared that he never intended to stop talking to her for me or anyone else.

After much prayer and many tears, I filed for a separation. When John received the papers, he was furious. I did not know what to expect from the man who had already threatened to kill me and his friend; the man who escaped the justice of the law not once, but twice.

My brother feared for our lives and sent me and my youngest daughter to my family in Jackson Mississippi, to get away for a while. Things did cool down.

"So I say to you, ask, and it will be given to you; seek, and you will find; knock, and it will be opened to you. "For everyone who asks receives, and he who seeks finds, and to him who knocks it will be opened.

Luke 11:9-10

I asked and being the attentive Father that He is, He answered. How wonderful it is to know that nothing is too small or too big for Him!

Chapter Six

The Angel in the Limo

*W*hen we returned home, I found out that I did not have a car for the summer. According to John, it was in the shop. Without a car, I could not work at the summer program. I needed that income. I was in a desperate situation. Filing for separation, fearing for my life, financially stressed and now, no car. I prayed and asked God if I could please at least have a car during all of this.

One day the phone rang, someone from Church called and asked what I was doing, I responded nothing really, but that I had been praying to have a way to get to work, but I didn't have a car. She asked me what time I needed to be at work. I mentioned to her that my daughter was working with me and would be riding as well. She said that was fine and that she would pick us up in the morning.

The sun was bright the next morning. My daughter looked out the window and said "Mommy who is this in this big fancy car sitting in front of our house?" I looked and told her God had sent someone to pick us up to go to work. My husband jumped up and looked out the window mad, we went to work in this beautiful car that my daughter liked to call a limo. This lady drove from Oakwood, Ohio to Cleveland every morning for two weeks, I wanted to call her an angel of God, because she made sure I was ok and had a ride to and from work and anything else I might have needed until my car was out of the shop. Angel had told me her husband was sick. I already knew of his illness. She told me that she had prayed and asked God for a little more time with him. God granted her a little more time. Angel's husband passed in October. Before his death, he asked his wife if Ernestine was ok. He did not even ask about his children, but was concerned about all I was going through. His wife told him everything was o.k. and not to worry. At the time of his funeral, I had stopped attending that Church because my husband was attending and was an Associate Minister. I made up my mind that I no longer wanted to see my husband playing Church. Even so, I went to my friend's service at the Church to see him for one last time. I paid my respect and said thank you.

"But as for you, you meant evil against me; but God meant it for good, in order to bring it about as it is this day, to save many people alive".

Genesis 50:20

"*Like Job, I was being tested and tried. However the Lord said no to the evil one and would not let him take my life! Looking back now, I know the LORD had a greater purpose for me in His kingdom.*"

Chapter 7

9-1-1

*I*n July, Joi our youngest daughter had gone to Washington, DC for job interviews. She had thought of moving away from home, in pursuit of a better job and to get some peace from the drama of the divorce that had filled our lives for what seemed like an eternity. She was tired of watching her dad play his various roles. He flowed in and out of each scene like a seasoned actor. He easily went from minister to hit man, from ministering in the pulpit to attending the needs of the other woman. It was all like a bad movie. She tried to block it out, but there was always something that nudged her back to reality, like the times her dad would start yelling and calling her disrespectful names. To him, we were both B's and H's. It was so frustrating and hurting to hear that kind of language coming from her own father. After thinking about it, she decided to leave for a week.

John found out about her plans. He was furious! He was upset because Joi didn't ask his permission to go out of town. He felt that she had disrespected him and when she returned he was going to put her out. Joi was 26 years old at the time. John went to the U-Haul company and purchased storage boxes. He proceeded to throw Joi's clothes into the boxes. He wanted me to help but I refused. John felt he was loosing control of Joi Joi stood up for what she knew was morally right. She wouldn't say anything negative about the situation nor would she egg on any wrong doing or go along with his plans. She would use the Word on him and warn him of planning and scheming evil against me. She would say, "Daddy has to pay for the wrong he's going to pay for his sins; I'm not going to hell with him".

On Friday, the day before Joi was to return home from her trip from Washington, I sat on the deck crying to

God. What was I going to do? I received notice that court would be cancelled. We were supposed to attend a court hearing that Monday, but his lawyer was heading out of town on vacation. While I was still sitting on the deck, I phoned a friend. She wanted me to visit her so that I could take some time to calm down. My husband came outside and demanded that I get off the phone. I refused. I paid the phone bill. He was already outside barbequing on the grill, but I ignored him. Later that day he came out to sit outside where I was. He said, "Remember when I told you to get off the phone and you didn't?"

Suddenly, he put a knife to my face and said, "I can kill you, and nothing will be done about it." I thank God that I did not move. I couldn't move. If I would have moved the slightest bit, I would have been cut, I let him have his say. When he put that knife down I went to the front of the house and dialed 9-1-1. The police came and took him to jail. He denied the whole thing.

John was still in jail when Joi returned home. Joi knew John wanted her out of the house, but God had him put out.

My lawyer and I went through the process through the courts to keep him out of the house (for at least three days).

When he got out of jail, the sheriff came with him to get his belongings. He took all the food out of the refrigerator and the freezer. He brought along our grandson to help him get everything out that he wanted.

Because of the knife incident, I went to court. I was represented by a public defender. John's original lawyer had a heart attack and did not survive. His assistant took over the case. They asked for a jury trial. It was my word against his. The jury found him not guilty. The judge told me after the trial that she knew he was guilty but when they chose to have a jury trial, it was out of her hands.

After the hearing, I could see my middle daughter shouting and screaming for their victory. It was like my heart stopped. I wondered why God let him get away again. It hurt even more to see my middle daughter rejoicing at yet another one of her dad's evil tricks.

I accepted my defeat and went home. Joi, my youngest daughter, comforted me. We went to the Word of God, II Corinthians 4:17, "While we look not at the things which are seen but at the things which are not seen. For the things which are seen are temporary but the things which are not seen are eternal".

My daughter Joi stayed with me for two years and went back to school to get her Masters degree in Psychology.

There were so many similar incidents with John, the court system and one set back after another. The divorce had taken a toll on Joi's grades. She ended up dropping out because her grades had fallen to a C. She could not stay in the Masters degree program with a C average.

Joi went to the Dean's office and told them what she was going through with me. He told her to drop the course for now. He also said that it was good that she told him because he knew something was wrong. He empathized with her, but advised her that dropping out and being there for me was the best thing for her to do right now. When things settled at bit, she could reapply to the program. She really wanted her Masters degree. She dropped out of the classes, but stayed there and worked.

"I have shown you in every way, by laboring like this, that you must support the weak. And remember the words of the Lord Jesus, that He said, 'It is more blessed to give than to receive.'"

Acts 20:35

"*During this time, I learned that it is truly a blessing to help others in need. There is always something that you can give, even when you think you don't have anything. It is easy for us to think if we're not giving something large, then what we do have to give is meaningless, which of course is not true*".

"You will find most of the time, all people want is a kind word, gesture or just someone to talk with..."

*"... **I** realized the Lord was healing me by using me to help others."*

Chapter Eight

Severing the Ties…

*N*ow, I was living at home by myself. This year I

ended up going to court three different times. Hoping and

praying that the courts would grant justice. I had others

praying too. My first court date was for the knife incident.

John wanted to make a deal with the court. He wanted to

be able to move back into the house. I told my lawyers no,

I could not see living in the same house as John as we

waited for all of this to get settled. My lawyer had the

counselor come and testify about what happened in her

office. As we waited, my lawyer was getting nervous that

the counselor would not show up. I looked up and saw this

lady with a long black mink coat coming our way. The

counselor told my lawyer that she came just for me. She

was willing to testify because John should not be allowed

to be in the same house as me, by the way he acted in her office. They later came to an agreement that they would drop the knife charge if John agreed to stay out of the house.

John would not help me pay any bills (he never paid bills) he wanted me out of the house. He knew I did not have money because I was paying the bankruptcy. I lived on $250.00 per month for that whole year. My lawyer finally stopped the bankruptcy.

My daughter did not want me to put up a Christmas tree that year because we had always had all of the family around the tree. This year it was just the two of us. . She did not want a tree up but I insisted on putting one up anyway.

It was a time of such peace. I used that time to talk to God. For that moment, I did not focus on all of the havoc the divorce had wreaked on my family. It was like a brief, quiet moment of peace in a long, brutal battle. I kept reminding myself that   it was God's birthday not ours, regardless of what was under the tree or who was gathered around it.

One of my friends called and said that she was going out to give Christmas stockings to the homeless people downtown. I wanted to go but I felt like I did not have anything to give. I decided to bake cakes and slice them for the Christmas stockings. That was my gift to them. It felt so good, in the state that I was in and with all of the things I had been going through, to give what little I had to bless some one else. The people were so thankful for the love and the items packed inside of those stockings.

My daughter and I went to church on New Years Eve. God really used her. There were deaf people there and we sat in the back. This lady went through the Church asking could anyone help with signing for these people, Joi got up and signed the whole sermon. I sat down in front of her. I could see how blessed the people were.

After the service, people came up to us, excited and joyful. They said it was good to see God's Word spoken in sign language.

Jan 10^{th,} 2003

I went to court and again, nothing happened. It was continued on to Jan 21st. I got there late. I had the time wrong. They were gone when I arrived.

You will keep him in perfect peace, whose mind is stayed on You, because he trusts in You.

Isaiah 26:3

"*I know God is keeping me, even in the midst of my turmoil. I am devoted to Him and through His unchanging love and mighty power, I will not be shaken. He is my perfect peace.*"

Chapter Nine

Daddy's Girl

*O*ften during the drama of a divorce, people take sides of one partner or the other. In our case, our middle daughter was definitely a "Daddy's Girl". In her eyes and heart, Daddy could do no wrong. One night, our middle daughter called me. She said, "Mommy, Daddy really loves you. He never cheated on you and one day you are going to realize that". It was hard to hear my daughter talking to me like this. This is the daughter who always defended her Daddy's actions. To her, he could do no wrong. However, I could not figure out why she was always so against me. What did I do? This was the daughter I gave birth to months after my first child. Her birth was definitely a surprise, but I loved her too. Was it possible that she could never see clearly when it came to me and her father because of this? Did she resent me or somehow feel that I loved my older daughter more? I could not take anymore of her conversation, it was too painful. I hung up the telephone. Because of all of the mind games John played, and the conversation with my middle daughter, my head started swimming. Was it all in my mind? Was I losing my mind? Was all of this just a bad dream?

Shortly after that call, the phone rang again. It was a former friend calling me to make a confession. She proceeded to tell me that she had gone out with my husband. All the time he was calling me crazy, filling my middle daughter's head with lies, he was taking her out shopping for Christmas lights for the house. Despite the news and the two very different conversations I had just had, I could do nothing but thank the Lord. I could see at that moment, that God cared for me so much to let me know He was in control. The Word of God says that He would keep us in perfect peace. I was not losing my mind. John was cheating on me, not just with Liz but others as well. I knew it all the time.

Keep me from the snares they have laid for me, and from the traps of the workers of iniquity. Let the wicked fall into their own nets, While I escape safely.

Psalms 141:9-10

The wicked may set traps but as for God, He has His own plan of escape!

Chapter Ten

Moving Days

I went to court again. Nothing happened. His lawyer continued to file a Chapter Seven to keep me from getting money. I was tired. I was financially strapped. I wanted to give up. But, I had gone through enough to know that the only thing I could do was wait on God. I was willing to trust God, no matter what!

May 18th 2005

This was my week to move. A friend and I went to rent a moving truck. We had planned to move some of my things into a storage facility. It was agreed in writing, that all John wanted out of the house was his tools. When we arrive at the house with the moving truck, John was there as well with a moving truck.

After one of our court sessions, I remembered his lawyer scolding me and telling me not to play games with John and to make sure he's able to get his stuff on May 28th. I agreed.

On that day, he had papers that stated that he had the authority to get EVERYTHING out of the house.

My son-in-law works for the police department so he was able to help sort out the two sets of documents. John's documents said he was allowed to get everything out. My document, that he signed said he only wanted the tools. My document said that his move out day was May 28. His document said his move out date was May 18. It was such a scene just waiting to happen. Two moving trucks and the police, it was just too much. My grandson and my daughter were in the house screaming because they were afraid of him.

I showed the police my papers that stated that John was not supposed to be present on my move out day. At the moment, we realized one huge mistake on the part of my lawyer. The court had never stamped any of my agreements. It didn't matter that John had signed and agreed, there was no official court stamp. I felt like I have been set up. John's documents stated a different date than we agreed and included that he got everything. Surprisingly, his documents were stamped by the Court.

Realizing that I had been the victim yet again, I chose to just give in. I could have had it all postponed. I could have argued deceit on behalf of his lawyer, but I did not want the scene that was slowly coming to a boil, to escalate. I told the police let him have it. It is just stuff and I'm not going to fight him over it.

The police could see that it was a set-up. He had the money to pay skilled lawyers. I was at their mercy, with what little money I had to pay for legal defense.

The police shook their heads and later commented that they had never seen anything like this before. This scene should have escalated to fighting and more court battles. I had no fight left in me.

I went back in the house to calm my daughter down. She was screaming frantically. I was able to calm her down and reassure her that God is watching this whole drama and that if we stand still, He will fight our battles. Besides, it was only material possessions. She calmed down. As she was watching t.v, trying to calm her nerves,

John walked past her and picked up the t.v., while it was still playing. Fire went up the wall. I still couldn't fight. I just held back as the tears continued to flow. My oldest daughter came over along with others to console me simply by their presence. We all knew not to allow the scene to escalate. We sat quietly watching John as he moved everything he wanted out of the house.

It was strange, we sat and watched as John moved everything he wanted. It was hard. I handled it when he had my son-in-law move out all of the furniture. It was like he wanted to evoke rage in me, but I sat quietly during his rampage. Just when I thought it was about over, my middle daughter who had always been on daddy's side found a box of my clothes. Our eyes met as she went to pick up the box. I realized that she really planned to take my clothes. I couldn't take it any more. I yelled for them to get out. My middle daughter and her husband picked up the box and went out. Both of them turned around and laughed at me as they went out of the door.

I felt raped by my own daughter. They had helped their father along with his scheme to leave me with nothing. Now, they even wanted my clothes. I couldn't believe all that was happening right before my eyes. I had just been ridiculed and humiliated before all of the people present. I thought to myself, what else could possibly happen?

I went outside to leave and my car was gone. Oh my God! After all I had tried to do to not make a scene there were dozens of people outside watching and whispering. People were shaking there heads in disbelief of what they just seen.

John took what he wanted and left the rest for me. All of the furniture of value was gone. I had no energy to remove the remaining things at that time. I went over to my oldest daughter's house to rest. I couldn't move. I just wanted to sleep. I slept until 7:00. I went back home to get what remained of my clothes and any furnishings John had left. When we went back into the house, it was filled with a gaseous odor. I called a neighbor and he checked the gas and called the fire department. The fire department came and shut the gas off. The fire official told me that if I would have turned on a light the house would have been blown off the block. When John took the stove he did not cap off the gas. It could have killed us.

I had to take a leave of absence from work because I was under so much stress. The next two days I continued to get some of my other things out of the house. After the scene on the weekend, everyone else was too scared to help. I did it by myself. My youngest daughter tried to help, but was too tired and it was often late when she got home from work.

John had given my middle daughter and her husband some of my things. He said he really only wanted his tools.

I found out later that he had a new truck and a new girlfriend. I also found out that the day after the moving fiasco, he was in Church, in the pulpit, like nothing happened.

On Monday, my lawyer called John's lawyer to inquire about the new documents. His lawyer knew nothing of any new documents. John was not supposed to be there that weekend. As usual, nothing happened. During this whole divorce, John had been able to do whatever he

wanted without any consequences. This was just the
beginning of the games.

May 17th 2005

After several disappointing court sessions and
cancelled sessions, I finally got a support order. It was for
$539.00 a month. They had to do something because they
found out that John lied and said that he had been paying
the house note per our agreement. He had not been paying
anything.

Somehow, God allowed me to pay what I could
with what little I had. I continued to stand on God's
promises and wait.

After the lie came forth, John's lawyer could not
continue to assist him by delaying the support order, but

they did continue to assist him in hiding his income to avoid paying me anything else.

I would mention things that I thought they were setting me up on, to my lawyer. My lawyer did not seem to see anything wrong, time after time. John's side kept getting everything they set out to get. I felt that I had no one on my side to fight for my rights in court. I wanted a second opinion. I wanted a new attorney, but I could not afford one.

My lawyer knew this and my case was always put on the back burner. To me, she was just going through the motions, they were calling the shots. When I would question her actions or lack of action, she told me she was just doing her job.

June 1st 2006

I was looking for a new place to move. I had looked at different apartments, but none of them felt right. A lady at my Church told me she had a place. I had a dream the night before and saw a house in my dreams. When I looked at the house., I knew that this is what God wanted for me. Thank God, I now had a new place to call home, that felt like home. Now, I needed a car that was dependable and could get me where I needed to go.

I asked God for a car. One Saturday, my youngest daughter confirmed what I was feeling. She said,, "Mommy open up the window we are going to get a blessing."

I felt, no one would finance me for a car and that if they did, I would have to settle for what ever they gave me. I desperately needed a car.

One lot did finance me for a car. That car ran off and on and, in and out of the shop for about two years.

So much had gone on in the long divorce saga. It was still hard to go past the old house. My daughter, Joi, would ride past the house on the bus and feel like screaming. I would go another route to avoid passing it. I had a fear in me. I didn't know what would happen if I passed by the house. It was all too soon, so I avoided it at all cost.

It was now summer. If possible, I would have just sat in my new home all summer. I wanted to rest from all that had happened. It was still far from being over. I wanted to reserve my energy and enjoy the present season of peace. I decided to assist in the teaching and education of the youth at our Church during the summer.

I enjoy working with the youth so much. It made me forget about feeling alone, down and depressed. The children bring a fresh, untainted excitement about life. I enjoyed every minute of it. It kept my mind off of worrying. People who knew the divorce situation would ask me how could I act as if nothing was going on. If they only knew! I had mastered looking one way on the outside; only God could see the hurt on the inside. I could carry myself all day around the children and friends I would come in contact with, nobody knew the real pain I was experiencing. As the sun went down each day, so did my mask. At night, I could feel the pain of all I was going through. I would sometimes ask God, "Why was all of this happening to me? Why is this taking so long? Why can't I fight back?" He would simply wipe away my tears and let me know, not yet.

I was hurt and wounded in spirit. I went on my knees asking God if I could just touch the hem of His garment. I yearned to be whole again.

*B*eloved, do not think it strange concerning the fiery trial which is to try you, as though some strange thing happened to you; but rejoice to the extent that you partake of Christ's sufferings, that when His glory is revealed, you may also be glad with exceeding joy.

I Peter 4:12-13

"*G*oing through is never a good feeling. However, I can thank God for my tests and trials because as the Apostle Paul said in Romans 5:3-4 tribulation produces perseverance, and perseverance, character and character hope."

Chapter Eleven

Tests...

*M*y middle daughter and her father share a strong

father/daughter bond.   My middle daughter is so proud of

everything her dad does. She was so proud to tell everyone

that dad had a new car. I continued to drive my old car,

when it was not in the shop.

I joined a prayer group. It helped me keep my mind

focused. I had so much on my mind with all of the divorce

drama. Keeping my mind was of utmost importance to me.

Two years ago, my daughter and I had taken a class.

At the time, I knew all of the answers. But when I went to

take the test, the paper went blank.   It was as though my

husband and his lady friend were on the paper in a cloud.

Everything I knew drained out of me. I could not remember any of the test answers. I failed the test and had to wait another year to retake it. I learned to guard my mind and not to let John or anyone else take my mind. The prayer group helped me stay focused and realize that it is not about me, but about my representing the God I serve and that my job is to give Him glory in all that I do regardless of what people do to me. This year, I passed the test.

My daughter was still living with me, waiting to get money to get back in school.

September 23rd

I was visiting at my oldest daughter's house, when my middle daughter called. Their father had told my middle daughter to announce to them that they have an older brother. In my shock and surprise, laughter came out. What else could I do.? I could see God's hand in it all.

When I waited and refused to fight back or stand up for myself, God allowed everything that was hidden to come to light.

I found a new Church to join. I really enjoyed it, but I was never able to talk to the pastor about what I was going through with the divorce and the court system. I needed someone to talk to. There was no one. The deacon and the pastor were busy. I was crying out for counsel and I never received it. I stayed there two years. I eventually got to talk to every minister there, but never the pastor. I even talked to his wife but unfortunately she was sick and I could not burden her with my problems.

One day my friend asked me to go visit a church. I attended. I could feel right away, that this was a place I needed to stay. There was so much love there and I kept coming back until I became a member. God confirmed in my spirit that this was the place I was supposed to be at.

My eldest daughter was getting married. Even with all that was going on with the divorce, I always taught my daughters to respect their father. It did not matter what went on between us, he really did love them. One day she saw him in a store, he didn't see her behind him until the cashier told him, "You look just like the lady behind you". He looked back in surprise, spoke abruptly and ran out of the store. His actions hurt her so bad, she asked her paternal grandfather to give her away at the wedding. It worked out perfectly. Some people thought it would be a disastrous event, but with prayer, it turned out to be a blessed day. I was so happy for my daughter, but this whole incident added to John's anger towards me. During this time, he was mad at anyone that spoke to me. He cursed his brother out because he continued to talk to me. He felt like his brother should be on his side. His brother told him that whatever was happening was brought on by his own actions.

May 12, 2006

The judge canceled court and stopped my spousal support check. They said that I was not in compliance.

October 1, 2006

There seemed to be a lot of working behind the scenes to make sure I did not receive any type of support. I often wondered whose side my own lawyer was on. Not only did they take away my spousal support, I was unable to receive unemployment well. In all, they took $8,936.00 worth of income from me. I had no money scheduled to come in until April and I was unable to pay most of my bills. On top of everything else I was going through, I was sick in my body.

This was a very hard time for me. The courts, John, my health were all adding to the pressure I was feeling. I also needed to take and pass a very crucial test for a job. I kept encouraging myself by reminding myself that God is able and that all of this was just a test. God promised to take care of everything; but there were so many times I was just plain afraid. Just as He promised, God took care of everything. Somehow my main bills and rent always got paid. After all of the months with no money from John, the courts finally gave me $360.00 per month in support. God kept proving his faithfulness. Despite all that was on my mind, I passed my test for the job! I praised God. The test was equivalent to an associate's degree in that field.

January 2007

The next time we went to court, I walked up on my lawyer talking to John's lawyer. Just by looking at how they were interacting with each other, I could tell they were working together. It was evident in the courtroom that nobody had my best interest at hand. I shared what I had witnessed between the two lawyers with my dad and my sister. My sister agreed to find me another lawyer and paid the bill for it. Praise God! I was so hurt and angry that I had paid a lawyer for four years and nothing had happened. There was no reason for this case to take so long. It should have been a relatively simple case.

I felt so much better. Now, with the new lawyer, I finally saw the inside of the courtroom. With the others, I always waited in the hallways.

During this roller coaster ride of what was my life, when one area went up, it was certain that another would go down. On my job, I moved to a new school. I thought the change would be good, but after a few weeks, I wanted to go back to the old one. On top of that, because I quit the childcare job, it took me from the middle of August to the last of September to get paid from the new job. I eventually had to enlist the help of the Legal Aid Society to get my money.

October 2, 2007

With so much going on in my life, I wanted to find my true purpose. With this divorce, I saw myself waiting, month after month while others decided my fate. I had long lost the desire to fight back, I just simply wanted it over. I wanted out of this waiting room. I decided to enroll in ministry school. I struggled in school. I was still physically sick. So many times during the first year I wanted to quit. My car was acting up and I had to pay for repairs I could not afford. During this time, God spoke and reminded me that when I called He would be there and that I should not give up.

October 13, 2007

I really needed a car. I decided that I was really going to step out on faith. I knew that the Word of God said that if I asked anything in His name that He would do it. I really needed God to do the miraculous on my behalf regarding a car.

My goddaughter and I went to a local dealership. I really believed in my heart that God would do it. I needed a miracle. I had prayed and prayed, and now I was going to step out on faith. I informed the car salesman of the amount that I wanted to pay for a car. With the amount I told him, he politely suggested that I look in the used car section. I persisted and told him that I wanted a new car. He was shocked at my persistence and the fact that I knew exactly what I wanted. I picked out a 2008 Camry. My goddaughter and I prayed he would come back with an approval and a great financing deal. God performed a miracle. I got the car I wanted. The dealer allowed me to trade in my old car. I was so happy, I cried. My God is so faithful. I didn't understand why He was making me wait so long and go through so much with the divorce, but when I really needed a blessing, God did it! My goddaughter and her children went to clean out my old car screaming, "Yes, yes!" God had promised me that everything that was stolen from me was coming back. The car came back new, just as God had promised.

It was spring break. I picked up the newspaper. God showed me how the judge and the lawyer were working together. There was an article telling the story of another person who had been going through a divorce for four long years! I was in year six.

Now with the new lawyer and the news I just saw in the paper, I was finally seeing some results.. I could not believe it. Six years had passed and the Judge was finally listening to our case. The article in the paper, made the judges and lawyers leery of dragging out any more cases to milk the clients for fees, knowing that people were watching and that they could no longer have their secret hallway meetings and play games with people's lives.

May 2008

Another court day came. I wasn't even surprised any more when John's lawyer e-mailed my lawyer to say he had another trial so he had to cancel and handle another case. The wait continued. It was nothing new. This divorce had so many surprising twists and turns that nothing that happened surprised me any more. I had no choice but to continue to trust in the Lord and wait. I worked summer school. God blessed me with the best summer job in my life.

God blessed me again to work in a quiet school with preschoolers. I loved the atmosphere. It was so friendly and peaceful. My pastor called and gave me a date for my trial sermon. It was September 20. The title of my first sermon was "In the Waiting Room". The sermon talked about Job and how he was humbled by the situations He went through and how he waited on the Lord.

October 5, 2008

I was ordained as a minister. I finally felt like I was walking in my divine purpose. I felt as though I was right where God wanted me to be at this particular time in my life. I was still waiting, but in a strange way content. I had witnessed God taking care of me in all of the ups and downs of the divorce. When I wanted to fight, God said be still. When I wanted to do something, do anything but wait, God said wait. There had to be something in all of this that I could use as a minister to help someone else. Was my situation over? No, but I had learned how to wait on the Lord. In fact, I was still waiting, but maybe, just maybe it was coming close to an end.

I went to court again December 2, 2008. I was excited thinking it would finally be over soon. My hopes were soon dashed. The judge threw out my case because of some document neither lawyer had filled out. My heart sunk. I wanted to scream or just simply pass out. My lawyer and I talked for a brief moment. As I left the courthouse yet again, confused and feeling defeated, I felt a strong cold wind. The opposition I had been facing inside the courthouse was just as strong and cold as the wind I encountered on the outside.

My lawyer called me a little while later and asked me to come to his office. He had reviewed the court files and showed me how John had been hiding money and took everything from me. He also showed me how his lawyers had tried to cover it all up. Even with this new evidence, I felt like there was nothing really for me to gain bringing it up in court. . The judge was finally tired of all of this and wanted us to settle. He told me that if we did not settle this case by the next court date that I would have to pay court fees. He laughed and told me that by the looks of it, I could just pay him now

I remember feeling God say "Move let me handle this". I really did not understand what He meant. I could not see where I was in the way. I questioned several ministers, leaders and bishops.   Most of them simply said I

would understand what He meant when I went back to

court.

One person asked me, "What was it that I wanted

to gain from all of this?"   I told her that I just simply

wanted the truth to come forth.   She told me that God

knows the truth and that I should just let that be enough.

She told me to not let my pride get the best of me. She felt

that the courts were not interested in anything else I had to

say and that at this point, the court was not going to do

anything about it. I kept hearing God say, "Move

Ernestine, let me handle it".   I did not know how to move

and get out of the way. I didn't realize I was in the way. I

found this passage in the Word, II Corinthians 4:17: "For

our light affliction, which is but for a moment, worketh for

us a far more exceeding and eternal weight of glory." Our

troubles should not diminish our faith or disillusion us. We should realize that there is a purpose in our suffering. Problems and human limitations have several benefits. They remind us of Christ suffering for us. They also keep us from pride and cause us to look beyond this brief life. They prove our faith to others. This scripture gave me comfort. I needed to give God the opportunity to demonstrate His power. It encouraged me to have the confidence that whatever the enemy stole, God was going to restore. Every time I was afflicted God was there. When I had no money, God was there. When the house was gone, God was there and provided me with an apartment. When I was laid off and my unemployment was denied, God was there. I had no money to pay bills, but God provided. God kept asking, "Do you trust me?" I decided that I was going to continue standing on God's promise and for as long as He had me to wait, I was going to be obedient and have faith. I realized that my trust and obedience is what God wanted from me. This whole thing was not about whose telling truth or not, it was about being prepared to fulfill the purpose that God had for my life. I had been going through for seven long years standing, waiting for the truth to come out. God said move, get out of my way. I didn't know what it meant at first, but now I do.

Be still, and know that I am God; I will be exalted among the nations, I will be exalted in the earth!

Psalm 46:10

"War and destruction are inevitable but so is God's final victory. At that time all will be still before Almighty God!"

Chapter Twelve

Allowing God to be God

March 5, 2009

*J*ohn went on the stand. I should say John went on

the stage. He played a pitiful act. He accused me of lying

and making him lose his home. (Wasn't it our home?) He

said I put him in jail for three days and that he never put a

knife to my throat.   He said the story of our middle

daughter and her husband coming on my scheduled moving

day and taking all of the things I was entitled to, never

happened. He said he only got a few clothes and his tools.

He went on to say, that I sold everything else. He denied

the story about the stove and the gas that engulfed the

house. He said none of it ever happened. It was all just lies.

He told the Judge that after I caused him to lose his

nice house, he was forced to live at Liz's house and drives

her car. Jokingly, he told my lawyer that if he talked to her long enough, she would let him drive her car too. He lied about his taxes, about doing construction jobs for people. He told the Judge that he occasionally changed a few light bulbs and painted a house.

After all of John's tall tales, it was my turn to take the stand. I went to the stand with a piece of paper that listed dates and events. His lawyer snatched the paper from me. I was so nervous. I needed the piece of paper to remember certain dates. He used my nervousness to try to make me look like a fool. He tried to paint a picture of John being a good father, a faithful minister, a caring family man and God bless America, a veteran.

John continued on with his act. He lowered his head and covered his face. His lawyer scowled and pointed his finger at me, and said "God is going to get you for what you did to my client."

It was all too much. It was a long day in court. I was glad when it was over. Unfortunately, it was not really over. I left the court torn, but even so, I felt a load had lifted off of my shoulders. On the inside, I felt like something was taken out of me. It was like something was scraped out of me. My body was literally sore for days. Then, God said for me to start buying the newspaper. I really did not have time to read it but bought in out of obedience. It was amazing. Just one week from the time John's lawyer told me God was going to get me, I guess you could say God got him. In the paper, I read where his law partners wanted to have him disbarred for hiding money for his clients in other divorce cases.

Despite this news, our case continued on. When my lawyer had presented closing remarks. John's lawyer requested a fourteen day continuation, they granted it. One day after I was speaking at Bible Study about my life and my purpose. There were so many questions thrown at me. It even seemed like an attack. I knew it was the enemy's design to get me off track from where I needed to be and get upset. All the things they were saying and asking about, I remember what God said, "Hold your peace and wait, I will restore everything back to you". In my waiting, I had learned not to worry about material possessions. In my waiting I had learned to forgive those who had set traps and snares for my destruction. I forgave them all. I prayed for John, his lawyer, my daughter and Liz .I knew that God loved them also. I realized while we are waiting on God to move on our behalf, He gives us a chance to ask for forgiveness and works out some things in us.

I finally, got a copy of John's lawyer closing remarks. John, after all he had done, wanted me to pay support to him. I remember what God said that He would repay me. I had been living seven years paycheck to paycheck, (when there was a paycheck). My lawyer's closing remarks asked for spousal support; I just wanted my life back. When the judge finally closed the case, God gave me everything back. It was just as He promised. I trusted God with everything, to the point of walking away from it all and God restored it back.

God's capacity for restoring life is beyond our understanding. Forests, burn down are they able to grow back? Broken bones do heal. Our tears can be seeds that will grow into a harvest of joy because God is able to bring good out of tragedy. When you are buried by sorrow, know your times of grief will end and that you will find joy again. God's great "Harvest of Joy" is coming.

After seven long years in God's waiting room, the doors to new possibilities and restoration have swung open. Sometimes we think the healing begins when we leave the waiting room and are ushered in one of the other rooms. But in God's waiting room, the healing begins while we are waiting. It is not easy to wait. Waiting works out our patience. Waiting perfects our faith. Waiting builds our relationship with God. It is during this time of waiting that God is doing a work on us. When God's work in the waiting room is complete, then He will open the doors to so many possibilities in our lives that the time we waited seems insignificant. I pray for all of you who may be in God's waiting room. Be encouraged for they that wait upon the Lord shall renew their strength.

In closing, I want to encourage my sister or brother who may be going through such turmoil as I endured. It may seem that the other person is getting away with something. Always remember, whatever they have done to hurt you, God will turn it around for your good.

God knew my future all along. He is now allowing me to see a glimpse of it and it looks wonderful! I now see that I had to go through so many things, so that I could be qualified to help others. Praise God I came through the storm unharmed. If you keep your trust in the Lord, you will too. God bless you.

My Precious Jewel

My precious jewel that you are,
A virtuous woman by far.

Priced well above rubies,
You exceed your duties.

Not afraid of what is to come,
Your work is already done.

Planned and prepared
You are never scared.

Helping those in need
While raising your seed.

You multitask
And do as asked.

Forever grateful am I
My virtuous woman, I will imply

Clothed in silk and purple royalty
For all to see.

The beautiful queen
The groom's wedding ring

My precious jewel
And helping tool.

DeVonya Griffin
Copyright 2010

To order additional copies of, "In God's Waiting Room" or to arrange speaking engagements with the author Ernestine Carreker, please contact the Publisher at:

Parablist Publishing
P.O. Box 43379
Richmond Heights, OH 44143

parablistpublishing@yahoo.com

For other great titles published by

Parablist Publishing House

www.parablistpublishinghouse.com

Made in the USA
Charleston, SC
23 June 2010